The 'One Book One Tree' logo ensures that with every purchase a tree is planted in countries affected by rising temperatures and climate change.

'One Book One Tree' provides local organisations with saplings to meet their target for tree plantation. Most fail to meet their targets simply because they do not have the money to buy saplings or even seeds. 'One Book One Tree' provides them with saplings and seeds so we can fight climate change together.

The Acorn & The Dirt is the first title in this initiative so thank you for your purchase and support. For more information please go to www.onebookonetree.org

Qalandar Press Ltd
Manchester
M32 8EB

The Acorn & The Dirt
Jacket layout by Melvin Johnson
Graphic design by Gul E Raana & Vassil Lakov

‘To reach its full potential the seed must surrender to the dirt’

Khwaja Shamsuddin Azeemi

The Acorn & The Dirt

written by Adnan Malik Azeemi
& illustrated by Amy Louise Smith

In a forest, up there, at the top of the tallest tree
Hung an acorn watching over all, happy to just be

Every day it saw the sun shine so bright
And the moon and stars dazzle each and every night

Up so high, the acorn felt so very blessed
Looking down at the busy forest, the acorn lay at rest

All the hustle and bustle so far down below
As the rain, wind and sun caressed it so

Then came a whisper; "what if this paradise came to an end?"
Without the stalk to the branch on whom to depend?

The connection so clear, what if the branch broke?
Within the acorn, fear and worry suddenly awoke

The burden of doubt weighed the acorn down
And worry sent the acorn hurtling straight to the ground

A crack, a jolt and the grave unspeakable fear
Gripped by such, into the depths the acorn disappeared

Down, and down and down the acorn fell
How far down the acorn could not tell

With a bump the acorn hit the dusty earth
And with bruised pride the acorn held on to its worth

Up leapt the dirt as the acorn hit the ground
Upon the gentle breeze the dirt swirled all around

Another doubt-ridden seed that must learn how to grow
Another fearful acorn that must learn to let go

"Why am I here? I belong up there!
To live my life without a care!

"Here I am, alone in the dirt!"
Shouted the acorn, wounded and hurt

Then the dirt spoke, the sweet soft mud
Upon whom the acorn had fallen with a deep, heavy thud

“Stop your moaning, everything is just right
Don’t try and fight it, try as you might”

"Fight it? I wouldn't know how!
Up! - I need to get back there, right now!"

"From up on high you have been sent here
Cool your boots, you have nothing to fear"

“Nothing to fear? I’ll be eaten alive
I have no clue what to do, or how to survive”

“You have nothing to do, nothing to fear
It is your destiny to be right here”

“Then tell me, o dirt, why am I on the ground?
Where all the fallen are to be found?”

“To achieve your purpose, you must surrender to me
Only then can you be all that you might be”

"Surrender to you? But you are beneath me!
Why am I down here? How could this be?"

"I am beneath all, and from whom all is grown
It is in the dirt that seeds are sown

"Relinquish your shell, let it fall away
And soon you'll be a great tree one day"

"A tree? Me? That will never be!
This destiny is far, far beyond me!"

"When fear awoke that is when your branch broke
Now beware your fear of failure, and its invisible cloak

"For if you wish to return to that tranquil paradise
You must overcome fear, and not think twice"

The acorn regarded the tall, giant tree
Whom had held it so high, and so tenderly

Who had kept it nourished, safe and secure
The acorn viewed the tree with longing and awe

“I cannot release my shell, I’ll be vulnerable and exposed”
To the prospect of being a tree, the acorn was firmly opposed

“If you stay as you are, you won’t last long
As a meal for the birds will be your last song

“Or tucked away for a winter’s feast
Just another tasty meal for a woodland beast

“But if you surrender and accept your fate
You will grow tall and return to that heavenly state

"Where every day you saw the sun shine so bright
And the moon and stars dazzle each and every night

"With the hustle and bustle so far down below
With the rain, wind and sun caressing you so"

"But look at this tree, how could it be?
That maybe one day, this could be me?"

"Don't concern yourself with the how, or the why
Make your intention, be brave, and give it a try"

"But without my shell I'll be naked, afraid
What if I can't do it? What if I can't make the grade?"

"Most acorns never again see the light of day
Because, just like you, they thought the same way

"The choice is yours; surrender to me; or to fear, in defeat
Become a tree; or a squirrel's breakfast treat"

Longing for the past, the acorn remained too scared to try
Even if in the belly of a beast it would definitely die

"To deliver you to the present is the purpose of the past
Wallow in grief for yesterday and this moment will pass

"For heaven is simply a state of mind
It is not up there nor too hard to find

"But before you decide, first have a taste
Of this dirt scattered all over the Earth's face"

Believing no harm, the seed took a bite
And its heart ripped open with abundant delight

Fears and worries swept away
Unending bliss, come what may

The acorn realised it could not delay
As gratitude grew for such an auspicious day

"Why, oh why didn't you say this before?
After just a taste there's nothing I want more!"

"Then don't waste a moment, don't hesitate
In love, submit, surrender, yourself annihilate"

In loving devotion, the acorn's shell fell away
Alone in the dirt the seed with longing did pray

The dirt pulled the seed into a loving embrace
For deep in the dirt was the seed's rightful place

Annihilated by dirt, the seed had surrendered
Deep in the earth was heaven remembered

The dirt unlocked the secrets hiding within
And so the seed's journey did truly begin

Now it's your turn to become part of the story. It's easy, all you have to do is plant a tree.

Anything done with love and care is certain to succeed, so plant a tree and watch it grow and blossom over the years to come. We wish you the best of luck!